GOD MADE ME

by Debra K. Stuckey

illustrated by Kathy Mitter

CONCORDIA®

Publishing House
St. Louis

God made my feet.
Step, step, step, I go to church.

God made my hands.
    Clap, clap, clap, I praise Him.

God made my mouth.
La, la, la, I sing for Him.

God made my nose.
Sniff, sniff, sniff, I smell His flowers.

God made ALL of me!

I am His and He loves me,

just the way I am.